Reviewers Comments

"SUICIDE: WHY? is comprehensive and informative - answers the questions a lay person has about suicide." Ann Marshall, Burnsville, MN.

"Ms. Wrobleski is not an alarmist, but a realist committed to helping us move beyond denial to recognition and response. She continues to encourage us, indeed, demand from us, that we learn more about the facts of suicide, the warning signs and avenues for prevention." Rev. Richard Gilbert, Burlington Medical Center, Burlington, IA.

"You express yourself very clearly. The questions asked are ones I asked. SUICIDE: WHY? flows well, and is very readable. I liked that you did not skirt any tough questions, and are not afraid to revisit your pain." Shirley Lieberman, mother of daughter who died by suicide, St. Paul, MN.

SUICIDE: WHY? should be in the hands of every person. In an intriguing question-and-answer format, Wrobleski dispels the myths about suicide and urges the removal of the taboo and stigma that for so long has kept society from preventing this final act of desperation." Ruth Messinger, the American Funeral Director magazine, New York.

"I liked SUICIDE: WHY? very much, and the information was easy to understand. I wish I'd had it after my son died when I was desperately searching for answers. I'm glad your book will be available to help other suicide survivors." Sharon Goetzke, mother of son who died by suicide, Wayzata, MN.

NEW ADDRESS AND PHONE
Adina Wrobleski
2615 Park Ave, Suite 506
Minneapolis, MN 55407
612-871-0068

PRE

We must light the dark corners of taboo and stigma. We must silence the loud voices of ignorance.

Adina Wrobleski

SUICIDE: WHY?

85 Questions and Answers About Suicide

SUICIDE: WHY?

85 Questions and Answers About Suicide

Adina Wrobleski
AFTERWORDS
Minneapolis

Copyright © 1989 by Adina Wrobleski.

Cover and book design: Susan Lasley

Published by:

Adina Wrobleski
AFTERWORDS
5124 Grove Street
Minneapolis, MN 55436
(612) 929-6448

Printed in the United States of America.
First Edition 1989

PUBLISHERS CATALOGING IN PUBLICATION DATA

Wrobleski, Adina
   Suicide: Why? 85 Questions and Answers About Suicide

Includes bibliographical references, index, helpful organizations
1. Suicide - North America.
2. Mental Illness. 3. Psychiatry.
4. Psychology. I. Title.

Library of Congress Catalog Card Number:
89-80314

ISBN 0-935585-03-6

PRE

To my husband, Hank, to my family, to all the people who helped me along the way, and in memory of Lynn Wrobleski Oja.

TABLE OF CONTENTS

Numbers • rates • who • men • women •
• warning • courage or coward • drinking,
smoking • notes • methods • revenge • homicide-
suicide

Young people • "bad" parents • rock music,
satanism • imitation • evidence • romanticizing •
• pacts

Religion • taboos • funeral rites • opinions •
• rational • suicide • advocates of suicide • choice

Behavior • trying to get attention • suggestion •
• dangerous thinking • love and understanding •
• hotlines • chief danger sign • danger signs

What doesn't cause suicide? • substance abuse •
• causes of suicide • mental illness • causes of
mental illness • chemical imbalance • psychosis •
• inheritance • learning • state of mind

About The Author

Adina Wrobleski is a suicide survivor. Her daughter, Lynn Wrobleski Oja, killed herself on August 16, 1979.

The grief and frustration of that tragedy began the unfolding of a new and remarkable career - Wrobleski is today internationally known as a professional speaker and writer specializing in public education about suicide and suicide grief. She's published academic articles* and books for professionals and the general public.

Wrobleski's special writing talent puts complicated information into understandable and simple words. She lives in Minneapolis and travels extensively speaking and doing programs in the United States and Canada. Wrobleski is altruistic, ambitious and evangelistic in her crusade to bring light to the darkness that has cloaked suicide for so long.

* Her research articles on suicide survivors appeared in <u>Omega, Journal of Death and Dying</u>; <u>Death Studies</u>; and the <u>Israel Journal of Psychiatry</u>.

ACKNOWLEDGMENTS

In the past, I have regarded acknowledgment pages as a perfunctory listing of names of people somehow related to the book. I know now there is great emotion and gratitude that lies behind these listings. I feel very grateful to the following people who read my manuscript, critiqued it, gave me the gift of a reworded sentence, made suggestions, and offered kind words of encouragement. They are: Floy Brackey; Fr. John Catoir; Rev. Richard Gilbert; Sharon Goetzke; Earl Grollman, D.D.; Shirley Lieberman; James Lucas; Ann Marshall; Grant R. McKenzie, F.D., C.F.S.P.; Ruth Messinger; Nancy Rodman; Andrew E. Slaby, M.D., Ph.D, M.P.H.; Barbara Szutz, and Wasena Wright, Ph.D.

I want especially to thank Daniel Lee Menken, Ph.D, who is my friend and edited this book; it is much better because of him. And finally, my deep gratitude goes to Rodger C. Kollmorgen, M.D., Ph.D., J.D., who is my friend and was my psychiatric consultant on this book.

Preface

SUICIDE: WHY? is a book is for:

- the general public - education about an occurrence that for too long has been shrouded in shame and stigma
- caregivers and professionals - for themselves, and as resources for their clients and patients
- suicide survivors - people grieving the death of a loved one and searching for answers

SUICIDE: WHY? is in an easily read question-and-answer format. Readers may go directly to the area of most interest, or read all the questions to get an overview of the most recent knowledge about suicide.

The premise of **SUICIDE: WHY?** is that our best response to suicide is education, knowledge and commitment - only then can we prevent the spread of suicide, and comfort its survivors when it does occur.

Minneapolis, September 1989

Chapter 1

SUICIDE: THE FACTS

*"...Most suicide is a dreary and dismal wintry storm within the mind,
where staying afloat or going under is the vital decision being debated."*

Edwin Shneidman

How many completed suicides are there in the United States and Canada?

Every year about 30,000 suicides are reported in the United States, and about 3,500 in Canada. The actual number may be higher due to under-reporting. Men kill themselves four times more often than women.

About one million people worldwide kill themselves each year. It is difficult to find out about completed suicides worldwide because many countries have poor to nonexistent record keeping. Suicide occurs wherever there are people.

What is a "suicide rate"?

The suicide rate measures the number of suicides per year, and is used as a basis for comparison. It is based on the number of suicides per 100,000 people in the population. The United States rate stays around 12, and the Canadian rate is about 15 from year to year.

They vary between men and women, young and old and by race. Rates vary between states and provinces, but they are higher on the west coasts and lower on the east coasts of each country. Rates vary from country to country. The country that has consistently recorded the highest suicide rate in the world is Hungary (48.0).

Other countries that have high suicide rates are Denmark (31.6), Switzerland (25.7), West Germany (20.9) and France (17.2). Greece has the lowest rate (2.9), followed by Spain (4.1) and Ireland (4.9). This variance is accounted for by genetic, biological, psychological and sociological factors.

Do only "bad" people kill themselves?

No. Both "nice" people and "bad" people kill themselves and suicide occurs in both "nice" and "bad" families. In a foolish attempt to prevent suicide, long ago society placed a taboo and stigma on people who attempted or completed suicide, and on their relatives.

A taboo is society's way of censoring something it decides is so awful that people are forbidden to talk or learn about it. A stigma is the mark of shame and embarrassment placed on people who break the taboo. As a result, placing blame for suicide became common. Blame is placed on various people, situations and social institutions; blame is often placed on parents, on marital strife, chemical abuse and the "terrible times" we live in.

Who are the people who kill themselves?

Suicide in North America is a white and male phenomenon. Two-thirds of all suicides each year are committed by white men over 35 years-old. White and minority men represent about 75% of all suicides; however, minority men and women together represent only about 10% of the total each year.

Young white males have a suicide rate of about 19, while men in their 70s and older have rates of 37 to 45. The rates for older men have been declining since the 1930s when rates were as high as 80 per 100,000. Suicide among white people increases with age. Young minority males have high rates, but suicide rates decline for minority groups as they get older.

Do women make more suicide attempts than men?

Yes. Women attempt suicide three times more often than men, but men kill themselves four times more often than women. This is possibly because women and men are socialized differently. Women ask for help more easily than men - even in the form of a suicide attempt.

Women are also more likely to ask for professional help. Men, on the other hand, are expected to "tough things out" and "solve their own problems." Women also have traditionally used less deadly suicide methods than men. Increasingly, however, women are using guns to kill themselves.

At any given time one in every twenty people have depression or manic-depression. One in four women, and one of eight men will have depression in their lifetimes. It is thought that women are more prone to these diseases than men, but it also may be that they seek help more.

Does suicide happen without warning?

No. It often seems that way to the people left behind, but as they look back, they recall clues and warnings they overlooked or were afraid to see at the time. Society, however, has not taught the public or professionals what these clues and warnings are, nor what to do when they see or hear them.

Consequently, when the danger signs of suicide are seen or heard, fear and denial are the common reactions; denial may be the only psychological protection people have. Although there are exceptions, suicide is usually the end of a long process. Someone said, "Every suicide has a history."

Do suicidal people cover up how they feel inside?

Yes - to themselves and others. Most often they don't know where the raging, desperate feelings they have come from, and do their best to cover up and try to act "normally." On a much smaller scale, we can understand this by recalling times we went to work with the flu, and carried on as usual without commenting on how we felt.

Most people have also had the experience of being in a heated, angry argument with someone - they are red in the face and terribly upset - when the phone rings. They cover up their angry emotions, and answer with a calm and friendly "Hello." Suicidal people cover up their strong emotions too - sometimes up until the moment they kill themselves.

Does it take courage to kill oneself, or is suicide a coward's way out?

Neither. People who are contemplating suicide are not debating large issues of right and wrong, nor are they facing life bravely or "slinking off" to die. The desperate anguish that results in suicide is not "taking the easy way out." Cruel jokes are sometimes made and angry words said about suicides and their loved ones.

There would be an uproar if the same were said and done about any other death. Dying from pneumonia is not cowardly or courageous; neither is suicide. The taboo causes people to look at suicide as a moral issue rather than a health issue.

Are smoking, drinking, overeating and drug abuse methods of suicide?

Not really. There are two kinds of self-destructive behavior: direct and indirect. Smoking, drinking, overeating and drug abuse are indirect self-destructive behaviors. One person called them "chronic suicide," because they undermine health over a long period of time. Direct self-destructive behavior leads to immediate death.

There are also high risk takers - people who drink and drive, or ride motorcycles without helmets in disregard for their safety and that of others. In contrast are people who do sky-diving, mountain climbing and drive in high speed races, because they take elaborate safety measures to protect themselves and others.

How many people leave suicide notes and why?

In the days when the stigma was heavier, suicide notes were routinely destroyed so the death could be attributed to other causes. At one time, coroners declared a suicide death only if the person left a note.

Only about one-third of the suicides leave notes. Researchers expected to find clues and explanations from suicide notes, but studies over many years have shown that suicide notes are not particularly insightful. One expert thinks if a suicidal person could write a meaningful note, he would not have to kill himself.

Suicide notes fall into four categories. Most are loving communications asking forgiveness and understanding. Some are angry and hateful and directed at particular people. Some mix feelings of love and anger. Still others are sets of instructions about possessions and funerals. In this electronic age, suicides are increasingly leaving tape recorded messages.

Why do people choose the methods they use for suicide?

People who want to die choose methods that are deadly. Their choice is affected by the culture they live in and the methods available to them. Americans have so many guns, and they are so lethal, that over fifty percent of suicides kill themselves with guns.

In Canada, where there are stronger gun laws, about thirty-nine percent of suicides kill themselves with firearms. In South Africa guns are the chosen method for white people, and hanging is chosen by black. That's because whites own guns and blacks don't.

There are also some "suicide shrines" - places that somehow attract suicidal people. One such shrine is the Golden Gate Bridge in San Francisco, California. It is close to another bridge called the Bay Bridge, and yet a good number of people cross the Bay Bridge to kill themselves by jumping from the Golden Gate Bridge.

Is every suicide an act of anger or revenge?

No. Some people who complete suicide are feeling very angry - often at people near to them. This anger may or may not be justified. Others who kill themselves genuinely believe their families will be better off without them, and perceive their deaths as being a benefit. Still others feel abnormally guilty, ashamed and deserving of punishment.

A small number of people who kill themselves are delusional (out of touch with reality), and may hear voices telling them to do so. Nonetheless, all suicides are seeking escape from unbearable emotional pain. Some people kill others before killing themselves.

Why are there homicide-suicides?

Some people, usually men, are unable to sustain self-esteem unless they have constant reassurance, usually from the woman closest to him. This results in his being very dependent upon his partner - to a point that he drives her away with jealousy and constant demands for love and reassurance. His partner feels dragged down by a clinging dependency, and protests against it. When she finally rejects him, he kills her and then himself.

Other people have such rage that they want to hurt a particular person so badly they kill someone that person loves, and then themselves. Some people who kill their child, and then themselves, may have a delusion that they are protecting their child by taking him/her to a better place.

There is a chemical in the brain called serotonin, and low levels of a part of serotonin, called 5-HIAA, is associated with violence. In one study people who killed their child, and people who murdered others, were found to have lower levels of 5-HIAA than people who do not kill. The same low level was found for people who only killed themselves. About 4% of suicides are preceded by the murder of someone else - usually a spouse or lover.

Chapter 2

SUICIDE: AND YOUNG PEOPLE

"Why would anyone wish to end something as precious as life? To hate life, and to hope every day that every minute would be the last, to look at a little baby grow and to see the wonder of nature, and still want to die."

A suicidal young man

What is the perception the public has about suicide victims?

They, and their survivors, are viewed as "guilty" victims. The word guilt is virtually hyphenated with suicide. Even the language reflects this. Kindly intended people will say such things as, "Oh, it must be terrible for that family dealing with all that guilt," or "Oh that poor family; they must feel very guilty." There is no other cause of death that assumes a guilty complicity on the part of a family.

This has made it very difficult to form suicide survivor grief groups. In ten years these groups have not achieved a powerful national organization that charters groups or helps develop facilitators. By contrast, Mothers Against Drunk Driving quickly grew nationwide, and had a tremendous influence on legislation. Their victims are generally perceived as "innocent" victims of bad people.

Why is there so much concern about youthful suicide?

Teenagers kill themselves the least of all age groups, but get most of the attention because it always seems more tragic when a young person's life is cut short. Even though young people from 15 to 24 years old make up the smallest number of suicides - about 17% in the United States and Canada - their suicide rate rose quickly from the 1950s to 1980s.

There are various reasons why suicide rates went so high, but one of the strongest was the size of this generation. Social conditions are a factor, among others, in changes in suicide rates. The last time the youth suicide rate was as high as it is today (12 per 100,000) was in 1910. That was a year that saw the peak of another baby boom generation.

Do "bad" or "busy" parents cause suicide?

No. Good or bad parenting is obviously important, but it is irrelevant to suicide. To say bad parents cause suicide is like saying that only children of bad parents get cancer. Busy and career oriented parents who move a lot because of their jobs do not cause suicide.

There are many "bad" parents whose children do not kill themselves; there are many "good" parents whose children do. Our society has too often fostered the belief that suicide occurs in "bad" families - "bad and sick" families. Historically, blaming families and cheap talk are all society has been willing to spend on suicide prevention.

Does rock music, Dungeons and Dragons or satanism cause suicide?

No. A person who dies by suicide may be preoccupied with any one of these things, and after a suicide there is a human tendency to blame it on someone or some thing. Some music, games and satanism are very unpopular, and therefore are convenient to blame. People also look selectively at suicides.

They look at the suicides of people who were drawn to rock music, but not those drawn to classical music. They notice the suicides of people who played Dungeons and Dragons, but don't notice the suicides of people who played Monopoly. They notice the suicides of people who dabbled in satanism, but overlook the suicides of Bible students.

Are some auto accidents really suicides?

Yes. There are some claims that up to 75% of single occupant auto fatalities are suicides. There is very little research on autocide, but the studies there are indicate that one to five percent of these fatalities are suicides. It is usually not difficult to determine the cause of death when an individual uses a car as a suicide method.

In such cases the driver hit a fixed object with no evidence of skidding, braking or other evasive actions. The driver usually had a previous history of depression and talked about suicide. When there are alcohol or drugs as an added element, the risk to the driver is higher. Alcohol and drugs make people less inhibited and more prone to impulsive actions which includes suicide.

Is suicide imitated?

Possibly. It may be that a person who is already suicidal might imitate the suicide of a famous person, but even so it is rare. In the 1980s there was a lot of talk about a teenage suicide "epidemic," and about "cluster" and "copy-cat" suicides. There was more talk than action, however. People tend to be very disturbed by a few highly visible suicides. For a few days they talk about how terrible teenage suicide is, but then return to their previous unconcern.

From 1980 to 1985 there was a great deal of publicity about teenage "clusters" and "copy-cat" suicides. In that five year period, about 200 young people died in so-called "clusters." During the same period about 11,000 teenagers killed themselves quietly and independently without verbal or other concern. Two national organizations were formed to combat teenage suicide, but they had a brief life and now exist only in name.

Is there evidence that suicide is highly imitated by teenagers?

No. A single study in 1986 received a tremendous amount of publicity. It claimed that three fictionalized television programs about teenage suicide led to about eighty extra teenage suicides as a direct result of the dramas. Receiving no publicity were three other studies by other researchers who were unable to get the same results using the same methods.

The original authors, in fact, tried and failed to repeat their results, and admitted in 1988 that "The impact of the television broadcasts of fictional stories featuring suicidal behavior appears less widespread than we had originally proposed." Even after strong evidence to the contrary, the belief is still widely held by experts and the public that teenage suicide is contagious. (See "Summary and Research on Alleged Imitation of Suicide by Teenagers" at the back of this book.)

Is it possible to make suicide attractive, glamorous, and romantic to teenagers?

No. Some people believe that a teenage suicide should be virtually ignored. They often hold high positions and have advanced degrees so people assume they are right. These people say friends of a suicide should not be allowed to attend their funeral or honor them in any way. They say there should be no trees planted or memorials to them in yearbooks as is done for other teenagers who die.

This cruel advice is cloaked as concern for other teenagers. It resembles the old punishments of burial outside of cemeteries, trashing the reputation of the suicide, and banning and shunning the family. Out of forty million young people in North America 6,000 kill themselves each year. Common sense shows they are not like lemmings running off a cliff.

What are suicide pacts?

Pacts occur when two individuals feel life without each other is impossible and kill themselves together. Pacts are very rare and when they do exist, it usually involves an older, dominating male who has depression and a very dependent female.

In one study, of 68 pacts in a three-year period, 72% were pacts between spouses and 5% were between unhappy lovers. It is entirely possible that two people who have depression might gravitate to each other, feeling they are misunderstood by other people. It is also possible they may kill themselves together, but it happens rarely.

Occasional rumors have spread nationwide to the effect that twenty or thirty young people have a death pact, and that four or five have already killed themselves. It makes exciting gossip, and some may be titillated taking about it, but it hasn't happened.

What was the most notorious multiple suicide?

Four young people killed themselves by carbon monoxide poisoning in the same car in March, 1987 at Bergenfield, New Jersey. They each had a history of drug use and failure in school which are earmarks of depression in adolescents. It is not difficult to imagine these young people gravitated towards each other, but that four would die together is extraordinarily rare. Ironically, they lived in the state that has the lowest suicide rate in the country (7.5 per 100,000).

Chapter 3

SUICIDE: HISTORY AND RELIGION

"God of those who hope, look upon our brother tragically taken from our midst. Do not consider his sins nor judge him with the haste of a human heart..."

Proposed Catholic prayer for the soul of a suicide

Is suicide increasing because of the stress of living in the nuclear age?

Probably not. Each succeeding generation sees current conditions as worse than a nostalgic earlier period they recall. Stresses change with the society. One hundred years ago, there must have been extreme stress when there were no labor saving devices, and there was only physical strength to accomplish jobs. On top of all their other work, women had the added stress of having six or seven children.

This belief that we are living in the worst of times is echoed in this quote of an Assyrian tablet dated 2800 b.c. "Our earth is degenerate in these latter days. Bribery and corruption are common. Children no longer obey their parents... The end of the world is evidently approaching."

Do religious beliefs and taboos prevent suicide?

Yes. Catholics kill themselves least frequently, followed by Jews and Protestants. This does not necessarily result from a belief in life after death. Belief in punishment after death may deter some, but a desire for reunion with a dead loved one may be a motive for suicide in other cases.

In one study, however, Catholics killed themselves less than others only when they were the majority of citizens in a community. In general though, a taboo is an unhealthy form of suicide prevention, and takes a heavy toll in damage to families where suicides occur. Historically, the heaviest taboo on suicide was placed by the Catholic Church, but Jews and protestants were not far behind.

Do most religions give full funeral rites to suicides?

Yes. The major organized religions now realize that suicide is not caused by sin or the devil. They give compassionate and loving burial to people who die by suicide and care deeply for their survivors. Some religious groups still think suicide is a sin, but not an unforgivable one.

There are still some religious groups who treat suicides and their survivors in a harsh and punitive manner; fortunately, they are becoming smaller in number. Actually, suicide was not declared a sin until four hundred years after the birth of Jesus. Generally, organized religion recognizes that making suicide a sin hundreds of years ago was a misguided attempt at suicide prevention.

How did suicide come to be made a sin?

The early Christians had a severe problem with suicide, because many people were killing themselves in the belief they would instantly be reunited with Jesus in heaven. These were in addition to all the other suicides that regularly occurred. Suicide was made a sin in the 4th century in an attempt to prevent these deaths. The state also made it a crime to kill oneself.

Centuries that followed saw barbarous punishments inflicted on suicides and their families. To make it worse, suicide was made an unforgivable sin in the 13th century. Degrading corpses of suicides, confiscating their money, turning their families out of their homes, and burying suicides in unconsecrated ground was prevalent. It was not until the 20th century that the last statutes were removed that made suicide a crime.

Why do people have such misguided opinions about suicide?

The taboo on suicide prevented scientific study and education about suicide by decreeing that no one could talk or learn about it, and it remained in this forbidden realm for hundreds of years. Consequently, until this century so little was known that anyone could, and did, express opinions on whether suicide is good or bad, moral or immoral. One guess was as good as another.

Discoveries in this century of how the brain works and how it gets sick or damaged have advanced scientific knowledge about mental illness and suicide. People are replacing old beliefs and opinions now that there are medical and psychological answers and treatments.

Do people actually advocate suicide?

Yes. Some claim people should have the "right" to kill themselves, and that they should be helped to kill themselves if they are unable to do it unassisted. They publish advice on how to kill oneself, and print the names of drugs required. They insist they are humanitarians fighting for the right to a "peaceful death." Their typical candidate for suicide is a person who is painfully dying from cancer.

They stress only the extremes - the choice is between peaceful death or unbearable pain. They do not consider the fact that the pain of cancer is relieved by painkilling medicine. There is no evidence, however, that large numbers of cancer patients wish to kill themselves, but there is evidence that cancer patients who are suicidal have major depression as well.

Do rational and perfectly normal people kill themselves?

No. The mood in which people kill themselves prevents them from seeing any alternative but death. Many people believe suicide is a voluntary choice from among other options, but this is not true. The people who advocate suicide say we should "assist" people in their suicides by giving them the means and privacy to kill themselves.

They call this "rational suicide." They claim that people can look at the pros and cons of their lives, and "rationally choose" death. Proponents also say doctors should be able to give lethal injections to people who request death. These beliefs lead to ideas about the expendability of some lives which cheapens the value of all life in society. Rational and perfectly normal people, even in very painful situations, can see alternatives to death.

Why are there mass suicides?

Mass suicides are exceedingly rare; there are only two cases in recorded history where huge numbers of people died at the same time. They were at Masada in 73 A.D. where 960 Jews died, and at Jonestown in 1978 where there were 911 deaths. Both of these, and others where many people died together, usually occur in the context of defending religious or political beliefs.

In both Masada and Jonestown there were homicide-suicides as well, but the majority were "voluntary suicides." Voluntary suicides include religious or political martyrs who believe their faith is worth dying for, or that by dying one will go to a better place. The Jewish Zealots held their mountaintop fortress for almost two years, and believed death was preferable to conquest by the Romans.

Masada and Jonestown were also led by charismatic leaders who controlled every element of their people's lives. The Rev. Jim Jones of Jonestown, Guyana, was a man who probably had paranoid schizophrenia and certainly had total control over his followers: their souls, rituals, money, information, education, travel, shelter, and food. The people were in total isolation, and Jones held power through indoctrination, informers and armed guards.

Is suicide a choice?

No. Choice implies that a suicidal person can reasonably look at alternatives and consequences and select among them. If they could rationally choose, it would not be suicide. Suicide happens when all other alternatives are exhausted - when no other choices are seen. Everything has failed. It happens at the point of hopeless despair. It happens when they have one slender, last thread of control over their lives. If a suicidal person could choose among alternatives, he would not have to kill himself. The only choice or decision a suicidal person makes at the point of total hopelessness is to decide "The time is now!"

Chapter 4
SUICIDE: THE BEHAVIOR

"The biology of suicide is the biology of a behavior."

Shervert H. Frazier, M.D.

Is suicide a behavior?

Yes. One has actually to commit some action to hurt or kill oneself. There are degrees of suicidal behavior. Suicidal behavior is on a scale, or continuum, from zero to a hundred with only one hundred as death. Every behavior below one hundred is a frantic, and finally despairing attempt to find solutions other than death.

These include obvious behaviors such as threatening or attempting suicide, reckless driving, or abusing illegal drugs. These are often attempts to find solutions other than death for overwhelming emotional pain.

Most people who write or speak about suicide start with the danger signs, but that is almost too late. The danger signs are up around 95 on that behavioral scale. To reduce suicide, it is necessary to go back to 20 or 25 on the scale when the symptoms of mental illness first show themselves.

Are people who talk about or attempt suicide just trying to get attention?

Yes and no. They are calling attention to their extreme emotional pain and "crying out for help," but society has a callous attitude that says we should ignore these cries for help and pleas for attention. Self-destructive behaviors under 100 on the behavior scale are trivialized and declared "not serious." We get by with this indifference because nine out of ten people who attempt suicide never try it again.

Presently, we wait to see who of that ten actually dies before his behavior is declared "serious." People who talk about or attempt suicide need immediate medical and psychological help. They are "just trying to get attention" the same way people shout for help when they are drowning or injured in accidents.

Will talking about suicide give people the idea to do it?

No. If they are not suicidal, they will reject the idea. If they are suicidal, they usually welcome the chance to talk about their desperate feelings, and are relieved to do so. This is why most suicidal people talk about suicide before they do it.

Sometimes the words are indirect, such as statements about hopelessness, helplessness and worthlessness. The taboo and stigma affect suicidal people too. They hope someone will pick up their clues, which they may be too ashamed to make directly. Still other suicidal people make frank statements about suicide.

Is thinking about death or suicide dangerous?

It depends. Everyone has thought about his or her own death, which includes suicide. It is "normal" to have thought about one's own death. The truth is the majority of "normal" people have not thought about and studied suicide enough. Through study, experimentation and determination, death has been prevented or delayed for many life- ending diseases. This is not the case with suicide.

Death is the conclusion of life. As people grow older, they make provisions for their natural death; they make decisions about finances and possessions. This is "normal." People who work in the field of suicidology think about suicide a lot. This is "normal."

Thinking about suicide is dangerous when a suicidal person is not only thinking about suicide, but has a method available, and has planned where and when to do it.

Do suicidal people really want to die?

Yes and no. Until the point of absolute hopelessness, suicidal people are ambivalent about dying - part of them wants to live and part wants to die. They make various attempts to reduce their pain on that self-destructive scale from one to ninety-nine.

From their point of view, they have tried, and failed, at all the alternatives. The tragedy of suicide death is that a suicidal state of mind is temporary; if the person can be kept safe from himself - even forcibly - the mood will pass. The fact that a suicidal state of mind is temporary is the basis of suicide intervention.

Suicidal feelings may come and recur, but they always leave. Suicidal people feel hopeless because, although they remember that the feelings leave, they know that for them, they also return.

Will love, understanding and careful listening prevent suicide?

No. Being loved and understood, by themselves, cannot save anyone from suicide any more than they can prevent people from dying from cancer or heart disease. Many people believe that careful listening to suicidal people will pull them through a crisis, but people who are thinking and talking about suicide need medical care, not sympathetic listening from a well-meaning friend or kindly intended adult.

In a suicidal state of mind, a person's thinking is very narrow, and so focused they see only in black and white. They have so much emotional pain they are unable to think of their loved ones, cannot be reasoned with, and cannot appreciate all the good things they have in their lives.

Do hotlines prevent suicide?

Not directly. Hotlines are extremely helpful in intervention, but doubtful in prevention. Suicide attempters who are seeking changes in their lives - not death - are often helped through their crisis by a hotline. They serve a vital need for people in crisis, confusion, hostility and loneliness.

A crisis line listener is a phone friend who helps by listening sympathetically, and connecting callers with community resources. People who kill themselves have done all the reaching out they can, and have arrived at 100 on the suicidal behavior scale. Suicide completers plan it, mean it, and do it.

Some studies have shown that suicides do not decrease in communities that have hotlines when compared to those that don't. The fact is that the same thirty-five years that saw the installation of hotlines was the same period in which suicide rose so dramatically among young people.

Is talking about suicide a danger sign of suicide?

Yes. Most people who kill themselves have talked about suicide either directly or indirectly. Talking about suicide, statements about hopelessness, helplessness, worthlessness, and statements indicating a preoccupation with death are the chief danger signs that it may occur.

Danger Signs of Suicide*

In research done in 1984, 158 suicide survivors were asked about the danger signs given by 110 people who actually killed themselves. Here are the danger signs in order of their frequency. Note that the top five danger signs are all talking behaviors. The number shown is the percentage of suicides who said or did each danger sign.

Signs Given By The People Who Died	Percentage
Statements about hopelessness	72%
Statements about helplessness	68%
Statements about worthlessness	64%
Talk about suicide	57%
Preoccupation with death	51%
Were suddenly happier, calmer before death	41%
Lost interest in things they cared about	40%
Visited or called people they cared about	38%
Set their affairs in order	30%
Gave prized possessions away	15%

* This information was adapted from research by Adina Wrobleski and John L. McIntosh, Ph.D. published in 1987 and 1988 in Death Studies and the Israel Journal of Psychiatry.

Chapter 5
SUICIDE: CAUSES

"From the dark horizon of my future a sort of slow, persistent breeze had been flowing toward me all my life long..."

The Stranger, Albert Camus

Does suicide occur when a person feels better and has the energy to do it?

Maybe. The conventional view is that people do not kill themselves in the deepest part of their illness. It is popularly said that it is only when people start to recover that they have the energy to kill themselves. A more likely explanation was suggested by a noted research psychiatrist.

He points out that patients are sickest when they are in the hospital; while there, they receive 24-hour care, and daily attention from their doctors. When they are well enough to be discharged, they are recovering, but are still sick. They often leave with only an appointment in the distant future. In this period, "the mood fluctuations that frequently characterize the recovery phase of depression may be interpreted by the patient as relapse. Despair may ensue, and then suicide."

By themselves, do the times we live in, drugs, families, divorces or disappointments cause suicide?

No. Our external circumstances affect how we feel when we are sick, but they do not cause death. A big loss or a fight with a loved one just before a suicide is not the cause of the suicide, but it may be the trigger. Indeed, if breaking up with a friend, or having a fight with someone were a cause of suicide, there would be no one alive.

In their bewilderment about suicide, people often resort to blaming. They tend to blame what happens to them on the people around them and on social forces surrounding their worlds. In the aftermath of a suicide, blame is often attributed variously among relatives and friends. In the early 1900s people blamed suicide on things like how children were raised, and on the changes made in society by the automobile. Society still blames suicide on child rearing methods, and a new culprit - the insecurity of living in the nuclear age.

Does alcoholism or drug abuse cause suicide?

Not directly. Of the people who kill themselves, only 25% to 35% abuse alcohol or drugs. The majority of suicides do not. These substances are dangerous to suicidal people because they make them less inhibited and more impulsive. What happens frequently is that a person who has depression will try to make the emotional pain go away with alcohol or drugs. Then a vicious cycle occurs in which depression and chemical abuse feed one another, making both worse. The suicidal person then has two serious diseases. Too often the chemical abuse is treated, the depression is ignored, and suicide results.

Do people kill themselves less in hot, sunny countries?

Selectively, it may seem so. It appears to work that way in Europe where sunny Greece, Spain, Portugal and Italy have low suicide rates. Wintry Denmark, Finland, Sweden, Belgium, France and Germany have less sunshine and higher suicide rates. It does not work in the United States. There the sunbelt states have the highest rates, while the midwest is average, the south has both high and low rates, and the lowest rates are found in the northeastern states. In Canada, the warmer western provinces have high rates and the cold eastern provinces have the low rates.

There is a kind of depression called Seasonal Affective Disorder. Some people have a depression that starts every year in the darker winter months and lifts when spring returns. It is believed it has to do with a chemical in the brain called melatonin that is secreted only at night, and has to do with setting the body's internal clock or circadian rhythm.

What are the causes of suicide?

Suicide has its roots in the biology of the brain, genetic inheritance, psychological reactions to loss and environment, and social factors that affect all people. The brain is a physical organ of the body, and it can get sick in a variety of ways just like any other organ of the body.

Genes, environment, psychological reactions and social factors all combine to form the biological diseases in the brain that we call mental illnesses. The trigger for a suicide is usually the last thing the person was upset about, and it is the thing people are used to thinking of as the cause of suicide.

Losing jobs, failing in school and divorce are often said to be causes of suicide. These kinds of events are triggers, not causes, of suicide. Many people who kill themselves, however, have no trigger others can see.

Does suicide result from mental illness?

Yes. Basically there are three mental illnesses which may result in suicide. They are major depression, manic-depression and schizophrenia. Every year, about 10% of all suicides had schizophrenia and another 10% had manic-depression.

The vast majority of suicides had major depression, which most often was unrecognized and undiagnosed. Eighty percent of the people who have major depression can be treated successfully with medicine, psychotherapy or a combination of the two. This is the good news. The bad news is that of the people who have depression, only 20% get any treatment, and that fifteen percent of people who have untreated mental illness ultimately will kill themselves.

The remainder are suicides that result from anxiety and panic diseases, substance abuse, and a handful of "impulsive" suicides which may occur after a sudden catastrophic loss or disaster.

How many people have mental illnesses?

About ten million people in North America have severe depression, and another two million each have manic-depression and schizophrenia. From this pool of sick people come the 35,000 suicides that occur in the United States and Canada every year. One out of every twenty people will have a depression in their lifetime, and one out of every one hundred people will have schizophrenia.

As many people die from suicide as die from diabetes and liver disease. Both of those have huge foundations that raise funds for research, prevention and public education. There are national organizations that have the potential to play that role for suicide. They are listed at the back of this book.

What causes mental illness?

The causes are not well understood, but there have been tremendous advances in understanding how the brain works. We know today that mental illnesses are brain diseases. There are genetic, biological, and psychological causes for mental illness. People inherit predispositions or vulnerabilities to diseases both physically and mentally.

Psychology has to do with the mind and personality; biology has to do with the physical brain. There are chemicals called neurotransmitters and hormones of the endocrin system that regulate how we think, feel and behave. This brain chemistry gets out of balance when one has a mental illness.

What is a chemical imbalance in the brain?

The brain is made up of cells called neurons that pass on chemical messages about our emotions, our thinking, and our behavior. Each neuron is separate from the other, and the gap between them is called a synapse. One neuron sends a chemical message across the synapse to receptor cells on the next neuron, which passes it on the same way.

After the message has been passed, there is still some of the chemical message floating in the synapse that is taken back by the sending cell. When too much of some chemicals, or too little of others are left in the synapse, mental illness results. The medicines given for mental illnesses correct these imbalances.

Psychotherapy helps correct problems people have that result secondarily from the chemical imbalance in the brain. There is an additional unknown element beyond the chemical imbalance present in people who kill themselves, however, because only a fraction of the mentally ill ever consider suicide.

What does psychosis mean?

Psychosis is a state of mind in which people are out of touch with reality. They may have hallucinations in which they see and hear things that are not there. They may have delusions, which means being firmly convinced of something that is not true. For example, they may believe they have a fatal illness when in fact they do not.

People who die in squalor while there are thousands of dollars in their rooms often have the delusion that they are poverty stricken. Someone who is psychotic may talk in ways that make no sense, or withdraw into silence and immobility. Schizophrenia and mania are diseases that have psychosis. Most people who have major depression are not psychotic, but a few are.

Is suicide inherited?

No, but people inherit genetic predispositions to certain illnesses, such as major depression, manic-depression, and schizophrenia just as they do to heart disease and diabetes. One inherits predispositions to the diseases that can result in suicide. A history of suicide in a family makes one a statistically higher risk for suicide.

Although multiple suicides do strike some families, most others will have, for example, one suicide and then another not until two generations later. There will be many more cases of mental illness in the family than suicides, because most mentally ill people never consider it.

Suicide does run in families, and it is important for family health to identify the diseases it results from: major depression, manic-depression or schizophrenia. People need to recognize the symptoms and understand the illnesses in their families so they can get prompt medical and psychological help.

Do people learn suicidal behaviors?

Yes. Just as people learn other ways of coping emotionally from their families, they can observe and learn self-destructive behaviors as well. In about 20% of families where a suicide occurs, one will find other suicides or self-destructive behaviors. This is called learned behavior. A suicidal person may discover that threatening suicide gets an immediate response, and continue that behavior because it works.

This is called manipulative behavior, and it most often makes family and friends anxious and angry. Manipulation is usually scorned by other people, but it is really a part of the behavior that results from the disease. Suicidal people may have a combination of learned behavior and genetic inheritance.

What is the state of mind of someone who is considering suicide?

A small number of suicides are psychotic (out of touch with reality), but the majority of people who kill themselves are not "out of their minds." They are so focused on their terrible emotional pain, however, that they have a kind of "tunnel vision."

They feel absolutely helpless and hopeless. They can't call on their experience to help them. They cannot remember that moods pass - only that they come back. They are unable to think of alternatives to death, or of how their families will feel. Many think their families will be better off without them.

Just as people die from heart disease and cancer when they have "everything going for them," so also do they kill themselves. Wealth and loving families don't keep people from dying in accidents, and having "everything to live for" doesn't prevent suicide.

What is the illness that leads most often to suicide?

Major depression. There are two kinds of depression: endogenous and reactive. It used to be thought that only endogenous depression (coming from within) responded to medicines, and that reactive depressions (coming after an event) responded only to psychotherapy. This was also a way of dividing up the patients among health professionals.

The endogenous depressions went to psychiatrists for medicine, and the reactive depressions went to the psychotherapists for talk therapy. It is now known that even though a reactive depression may stem from an external event, the biochemical imbalance in the brain is the same. It is same illness, and its treatment is the same. Major depression is also called unipolar and clinical depression.

Chapter 6

SUICIDE: MENTAL ILLNESS

"Perhaps what finally makes him kill himself is not the firmness of his resolve but the unbearable quality of his anguish."

Albert Alvarez

Is there a double standard on mental and physical illness?

Yes. There is a particularly heavy stigma on mental illness, and it leads to some odd differences. There are a group of people labeled "former mental patients," but there is not a group called "former physical patients."

On those occasions when crimes are committed by people who have had psychiatric treatment, they are labeled a "former mental patient." One does not hear news reports that say, "John Doe, a former physical patient, murdered his wife today." People do not describe themselves as "former physical patients," though most people are. The stigma makes the difference.

Does "protecting" the civil rights of the mentally ill do more harm than good?

Yes. The so-called civil rights of mental patients has been carried so far that severely depressed and psychotic people are expected to use the same brain that is making them sick to make competent decisions about treatment. One man who has manic-depression pleaded that involuntary commitment be used earlier - before family finances, careers or reputations are destroyed during manic episodes.

At the present time, mentally ill patients in many states have a "right" to a hearing in court as to whether they need medical treatment. Judges, not doctors, are making critical treatment decisions. These patients have to be at the extreme edge of their illness - where they become suicidal or homicidal - before help is allowed. People are literally "dying with their rights on," and the way one dies from a mental illness is by suicide.

What is major depression?

Depression is a brain disease in which the chemicals that affect how we think, feel and behave get out of balance. It is a state of constant, unrelieved misery. People who have depression often are angry and irritable. They often are dependent to a point of clinging to, and dragging down people near them. Sleep, appetite and sex are affected. They are unable to feel pleasure about anything. Unless the depression is recognized, it is very easy to dislike people who have depression, and blame them for things they can't control.

Major depression is a disease that goes away by itself in most people, but usually lasts for a year to a year-and-a-half, during which time there is immense suffering. Antidepressant medicines take away the painful symptoms in two to four weeks. The treatment for depression is medicine, psychotherapy or a combination of the two.

SYMPTOMS OF MAJOR DEPRESSION

The following are a list of symptoms of major depression seen in the at-large population and in young people. Some young people who have depression do not appear unhappy and sometimes look and are treated as if they simply have behavior problems.

SYMPTOMS OF MAJOR DEPRESSION	SYMPTOMS OF MAJOR DEPRESSION OFTEN SEEN IN YOUNG PEOPLE	
Obvious unhappiness	No apparent unhappiness	
	Defiant	
	Rebellious	Various
Inability to feel pleasure	Disobedient	Acting out
Preoccupied with sad thoughts	Running away	Behaviors
Crying and tearfulness	Drinking or on drugs	Commonly
	Refusal to go to school	Seen
	Failing in school	
Irritable and touchy	Irritable and touchy	
Feelings of helplessness worthlessness and hopelessness	Feelings of helplessness worthlessness and hopelessness	
Withdrawn and isolated	Withdrawn and isolated	
Loss of energy	Loss of energy	
Self-neglect	Self-neglect	
Loss of concentration	Loss of concentration	
Loss of interest in surroundings	Loss of interest in surroundings	
Loss of interest in favorite things	Loss of interest in favorite things	
Physical complaints (headaches, etc.)	Physical complaints (headaches, etc.)	
Sleep difficulties: insomnia or excessive sleeping	Sleep difficulties: insomnia or excessive sleeping	
Appetite difficulties: losing weight or overeating	Appetite difficulties: losing weight or overeating	
Loss of interest in sex	Loss of interest in sex	
Thoughts of suicide	Thoughts of suicide	

Not all people who have depression will have all of these symptoms, or to the same degree. If a person has four or more of these symptoms, if nothing can make them go away, and they last more than two weeks, he or she should see a psychiatrist, doctor or mental health professional.

What is manic-depression?

Manic-depression is a brain disease whose symptoms alternate between the abnormal unhappiness of depression and the abnormal happiness of mania. People who have mania have feelings of extreme confidence, happiness and euphoria. They have grandiose plans, impossible goals, and unwarranted faith in their abilities. They go long periods of time without sleeping. They talk excessively and sometimes incomprehensibly.

People who have mania often undertake bankrupting shopping sprees or business deals, show excessive and embarrassing sexual conduct, and make sudden, impulsive decisions that result in trouble for them and their families. They may have delusions that they are omnipotent, have a special relationship with God, or believe they are another person. As mania continues they may become irritable, angry and abusive. After a manic period, they plunge to the depths of depression. Manic-depression is treated with a medicine called lithium, and sometimes antidepressant medicine as well.

SYMPTOMS OF MANIA

Extreme happiness, euphoria or elation
Excited, enthusiastic and agitated
Grandiose ideas and plans
Decreased need for sleep
Embarrassing social behavior
Irritable and argumentative
Over talkative
Speech doesn't make sense
Racing thoughts
Easily distracted
Extremely poor judgment
Can't foresee painful consequences
Overestimation of ability
May abuse alcohol to "slow down"
Delusions:
    Fixed false beliefs
Hallucinations:
    Hearing voices, seeing visions
Lack insight they are ill

What is schizophrenia?

Schizophrenia is a devastating psychotic brain disease. It is characterized by hallucinations, delusions, and speech and thinking that make no sense. Sometimes the person withdraws into absolute motionlessness which is called catatonia. People who have schizophrenia sometimes also have paranoia, in which they are very suspicious and may believe that they are watched or followed by hostile forces.

Even worse, people who have schizophrenia may also have major depression at the same time. Their suffering is enormous. Only powerful medicines called antipsychotics correct these severe symptoms. Schizophrenia is treatable, but usually is not curable. Some people who have schizophrenia do go into a remission of their illness.

SYMPTOMS OF SCHIZOPHRENIA

Hallucinations
    Hearing voices speak one's thoughts
    Hearing arguing voices
    Hearing angry, accusatory voices

Delusions
    Thoughts being withdrawn from their mind
    Outside thoughts inserted in their mind
    Thoughts are being broadcast to others
    Feelings being inserted in their mind
    Feeling one is controlled from outside
    Feeling a normal remark has a secret meaning

Thought processes impaired
    Vague connections between thoughts
    Markedly illogical thinking
    Unrelated words spoken as a sentence

Loss of visible emotion
    Blank facial expression
    Emotion inconsistent with speech

Catatonia
    Withdrawn to the point of immobility and silence

A diagnosis of schizophrenia is not made until symptoms have been present for more than six months, where there has been deterioration of work skills, social relations and self-care, and the disease appeared before the age of 45.

Chapter 7
SUICIDE: MENTAL ILLNESS AND ITS TREATMENT

"The common fear that drives a suicide is the fear that the situation will become much worse... The common fear is that the situation is bottomless, and that the line on internal suffering has to be drawn somewhere. Every suicide makes this statement: This far, and no further!"

Edwin Shneidman

Can one always tell if someone is mentally ill?

No. Major depression often appears to be unhappiness about problems in life and it is common for people who have major depression to go to school, to do their jobs, and fulfill their responsibilities. They may not look or act sick. Just as people carry out their responsibilities when they have the flu, so do many people who have major depression.

They carry their enormous pain invisibly as long as they can. However, people who have manic-depression or schizophrenia are usually known to be sick because their symptoms are so severe. They talk and behave in strange ways. The symptoms of almost all mental illnesses can be easily seen once one knows what to look for.

What are consequences of depression?

A failure in school, divorce or job loss is often named as the "cause" of a suicide. Various symptoms of major depression (such as irritability, loss of concentration, poor sleep, and the inability to feel pleasure) lead to disruptions in relationships in marriage, work or school.

To the untrained eye these symptoms often look like deliberate and willful words and actions - things the depressed person could change or stop if he or she wanted to. If unrecognized and untreated, these symptoms can eventually disrupt and destroy marriages, friendships, school achievements and careers. These end results are the consequences of the depression not the cause of the suicide.

Whom should a suicidal person see?

It is best to start with a medical doctor or psychiatrist. Medicines exist to treat major depression, manic-depression and schizophrenia, and only doctors can prescribe them. A medical assessment is also important because some physical illnesses, such as thyroidism, have depression as a symptom. In that case, it is not a mental illness, but a physical illness that needs treatment.

Only a doctor can rule out other physical illnesses that have psychiatric symptoms. After a medical evaluation and diagnosis, suicidal people often need help from a psychotherapist (talking therapy) to sort out problems created by their illness.

Aren't there side effects of medicines for mental illnesses?

Of course. The side effects of antidepressants are a dry mouth, constipation, difficulty urinating, and drowsiness. They can be handled easily by sucking on a mint, adding fiber to the diet, being more patient to empty the bladder, and taking the pills at bedtime. The body usually adjusts to these side effects.

As to manic-depression and schizophrenia, there are more serious side effects of antipsychotic medications. They range from weight gain to oversensitivity to the sun to the most serious of all, Tardive Dyskinesia, which affects about 20% of people who take antipsychotic medication.

Tardive dyskinesia consists of involuntary and unattractive movements of the tongue and mouth, such as chewing and sucking movements, pushing the cheek out with the tongue, and smacking of the lips. Another side affect is a zombie-like feeling and appearance due to the strength of the medications taken. Just as in heart disease and cancer, trade-offs have to be examined as to which is preferable: the untreated patient, or the improved, but still sick person on medication.

Do people have to take medicine all their lives?

Some will. Antidepressants are given for a certain number of months and then gradually reduced to see if the depression returns. If it doesn't, the gradual withdrawal continues until no medicine is needed, because the person is well.

There are mild, moderate and chronic depressions just as with other illnesses. Most people who have depression get well; some only stay well by taking medicine; and some are so sick they die. Many people are returned to health by medicines for manic-depression and schizophrenia, but most have chronic, life-long illnesses that require medicine to function at their best level.

People are used to mild and severe side effects of medicines for heart, diabetes and cancer, but frightened of medicines for mental illness. There are people who erroneously and deliberately say that medicines for mental illness are like illegal drugs. They are wrong.

What is electroconvulsive therapy (ECT)?

ECT is an effective treatment for major mental illnesses. It is underused because, historically, it has been wrongly associated with punishment and electric chairs. In ECT patients are given anesthesia and powerful muscle relaxers because ECT produces a convulsion, which is an intense involuntary contraction of all the muscles.

Electrodes are placed on the patient's head, and an electric current is passed between them that lasts for one or two seconds. This produces a seizure, which is a rapidly spreading discharge of nerve impulses throughout the brain. Typically a patient has ECT two or three times a week, and most people have twelve to fifteen treatments. The only side effect is memory loss - usually temporary. ECT is the treatment of choice for people who are highly suicidal, because it acts quickly. It is not known why or how ECT works, only that it does.

Does a suicidal person just need to talk things out?

No. There is a widespread belief that "getting thoughts out in the open" and "talking things through" are prescriptions for mentally ill people. They cannot do this, however, until medicine brings them to the point where they can benefit from counseling and support. The chemicals in their brains that affect how they think, feel and behave are altered to the extent that they can't reason and look at things objectively.

By themselves talking and "counseling" suicidal people has been tried for the last thirty-five years, and it hasn't worked. It is the same thirty-five year period that saw the 267% increase in teenage suicide. Mental illnesses and suicidal feelings are not something the average person can deal with.

What is psychotherapy?

Psychotherapy is a form of talking therapy or counseling. It is a treatment in which a person trained in therapeutic techniques helps people understand themselves better so they can make helpful changes in their lives. Psychotherapy is practiced by clinical psychologists (who have Ph.D. degrees) social workers with masters degrees, and psychiatric nurses.

Still other professionals do counseling, such as school counselors and pastors. None of these professionals can prescribe medicine. Psychiatrists are medical doctors who can prescribe medicine, and many also practice psychotherapy. The treatment for major depression is with medicine, psychotherapy, or a combination of the two.

Why do some people deny the connection between mental illness and suicide?

Society has wrongly assumed that people who have mental illnesses and people who kill themselves are "bad" and that they come from "bad" families - "bad and sick" families. This branding results in a stigma which is a mark of shame and "badness." There are stigmas on both mental illness and suicide.

Some people who work with the mentally ill want to "protect" them from the further stigma of suicide. People who care about suicides want to make it somehow "better" by divorcing suicide from mental illness. Both stigmas are due to ignorance, and both hinder treatment, recovery and suicide prevention.

Chapter 8
SUICIDE: SUICIDE SURVIVORS

"Ultimately, it is not so much how they died, but that they died. That is the tragedy."

Adina Wrobleski

What is a suicide survivor?

A suicide survivor is any person grieving a suicide death. A suicide survivor is sometimes confused with a suicide attempter, who is a person who tried and failed suicide. Suicide survivors are the immediate family and others who are grieving a suicide death.

Historically, and continuing today, suicide survivors are put apart from other grieving people. Assumptions are made that they have "massive guilt" and were somehow in complicity with the death. Families of suicides do not get the sympathy that other grieving people do. They are often shunned.

Should there be a funeral service for people who kill themselves?

Of course. Their life has to be celebrated and commemorated as others are. Their lives had happiness and love as well as pain. Pastors should be open about the cause of death, because it sets an example of the same love and forgiveness granted to others who die.

It also helps the survivors by getting the suicide out in the open so they won't have to tell other people one by one. Because of the taboo and stigma on suicide, survivors need more support and reassurance than other grieving people.

How can we help suicide survivors?

We can help by treating them like survivors of any other death.
Bring them food, offer to run errands, or help in other ways.
Express sympathy. Tell them you are sorry their loved one died.
Talk about the person who died. Give them a happy memory
you have of him or her. Be available. Go to the funeral.

Don't be afraid of suicide survivors; the worst that can happen is
someone might burst into tears. Put your arm around him or her,
and give comfort. Don't give into the embarrassment and shame
society imposes on suicides and their families. Reject the notion
that suicide results from "bad" and "sick" families. In most cases
of suicide, someone in the family was very sick and died. The
rest of the family is well.

Do all suicide survivors need therapy?

No, and even if they did, there are so many there would never be
enough counselors to see them all. As a result of the 35,000
suicide deaths every year in North America, 350,000 suicide
survivors are left behind. Consequently, there are millions of
suicide survivors in the population, and if they all were as
psychologically scarred as some say, they would be a huge,
readily observable, and deeply disturbed group in the
population.

It is frequently heard that one never gets over a suicide death, or
if perchance one does, it takes years. These are further punitive
messages brought on by the taboo and stigma on suicide. Grief is
not sickness, even when it is grief over suicide.

Is the pain of suicide survivors deeper and worse than other pain?

Probably not. It seems logical that each person can suffer only so much pain - that there is a bottom to pain where it can hurt only so much and for so long. There seems to be a randomness that more or less fairly assigns the tragic things of life to each person. It is almost as if there are quotas of pain. Some people have lingering deaths from cancer; some people have blindness, amputation and death from diabetes; and some people have the pain of suicide.

The extra pain of suicide survivorship is to know that society has not made the commitment that will drastically reduce suicide death. The people who felt the pain of cancer and diabetes banded together to reduce suffering and death from those diseases, and families and friends of suicides need to follow their lead.

How is power related to grief?

One suicidologist made the distinction that in any situation there are things an individual can do, and some that are up to others or chance. Suicide survivors frequently yearn for the imaginary power of changing the past. They go over and over events leading to the suicide, and dream they have the power that might have saved their loved one. But there is no power in the past - only the present.

While one cannot bring the person back, and while there are no second chances with the person who died, there are many second chances with the living. There is an opportunity to make up in the present what is desperately wished for in the past. The death of a loved one changes people; how they change is up to each individual.

What is delayed grief?

For various reasons some people are unable to submit to their grief. Sometimes small children are not allowed to show their grief, and some adults refuse to feel its consequences. Their sore feelings may lie dormant for many years until something triggers them and they finally succumb to their pain.

One person whose mother killed herself when she was very young wrote about the "rock" she had carried all her life. She thought it would grow smaller as she grew, but it did not. She carried it everywhere until one day when she began to cry for her mother. Her tears fell on the rock and it began to dissolve, and it grew smaller and smaller until it was gone.

Do men and women grieve differently?

Yes. People grieve in different ways, but North America has a feminine, middle class standard of grief. It says the "right" way to grieve is to express emotion through tears and talking. It is frequently said that women grieve more deeply than men.

Because the way most men have been socialized, however, they often are unable to show and express their grief. Not only that, but men are still expected to "hold up better" than women, return to work sooner, and to "be strong" for others. So when men grieve in the only way permitted them, or grieve in the only way they know how, society turns around and tells them they are "doing it wrong."

Do suicide survivors grieve the same way other people do?

Yes. Suicide survivors go through the same grieving process other people do, but because of the taboo and stigma they have extra problems. They have to contend with people who avoid them, or people who avoid talking about the person who died. They are whispered about and pointed out. Suicide survivors suddenly discover there are numerous "funny jokes" about suicide. They meet all kinds of people who confide in them that they too had a suicide in their family.

Suicide survivors who are open about the cause of death usually find their families and friends rallying around them. More and more suicide survivors want public memorials given to aid suicide prevention. There is a long way to go before society gives an adequate response to suicide survivors, but the public and professionals have started taking steps to reduce the stigma and increase education about suicide. There is reason to be optimistic about the future.

Why do suicide survivors survive?

Because they have to. One way or another, people do survive, and most people do it very well. Suicide survivors have endured times when suicides were buried with a stake through their heart, when the bodies of suicides were mutilated, and when society bankrupted and banished their families.

Survivors' lives are permanently changed by a suicide. They will never return to normal, but they will find a "new normal" as they rebuild their lives. Grief produces a huge emotional wound that hurts terribly at first, and from time to time throughout life. Suicide survivors survive and lead happy and productive lives. Despite the extra problems brought on them by the taboo and stigma, suicide survivors recover as do other mourners.

What can an individual do to help prevent suicide?

Learn the medical model of suicide: that suicide results from
mental illnesses and treatment is with medicine, psychotherapy
or a combination of both. Support community mental health
organizations with money and volunteerism. Write local, state
and federal politicians urging higher priorities and
appropriations for mental illness research. Talk about suicide;
learn about suicide.

What hope is there for the future?

There is considerable hope. There is continuing research on the
brain - on how it gets sick and gets well. There are improving
medicines and psychotherapeutic techniques. There is increasing
public education about mental illness and suicide. But nowhere
is there yet the emphasis and priority on suicide prevention that
is needed.

The public must demand that the professionals (doctors,
counselors, pastors, etc.) they deal with be educated about
suicide. This education is still too rare. Families of the mentally
ill and of families of suicides must take the lead in eliminating
the taboo and stigma which have brought such unhappiness to
so many people for so long. There is help and hope!

Organizations That Fight Mental Illness and Suicide*

American Association of Suicidology (AAS), 2459 South Ash, Denver, CO 80222.

American Mental Health Fund (AMHF), 3299 Woodburn Rd, #335, Annandale, VA 22003.

American Suicide Foundation (ASF), 1045 Park Avenue, New York, NY 10028.

Canadian Mental Health Association (CMHA), 2160 Young Street, Toronto, Ontario M4S 2Z3.

Depression: Awareness, Recognition and Treatment (D/ART), National Institute of Mental Health, 5600 Fisher Lane, Rockville, MD 20857.

National Alliance For The Mentally Ill (NAMI), 1901 North Fort Myer Dr. #500, Arlington, VA 22209-1604.

National Alliance For Research on Schizophrenia and Depression (NARSAD), 208 S. LaSalle St., Chicago, IL 60604.

National Depressive and Manic Depressive Association (NDMDA), Merchandise Mart, P.O. Box 3395, Chicago, IL 60654.

National Mental Health Association (NMHA), 1021 Prince St., Alexandria, VA 22314-1932.

* All of these organizations are suitable for memorial contributions.

RESOURCES

This book is written for the general public, and for caregivers and professionals - for themselves, and as a resource for clients and patients. Therefore, I did not make detailed footnotes. An exception is the alleged imitation of suicide by teenagers. Because this is controversial, a summary and citations from the scientific literature follows these resources. The following are some of the books I've learned from that have contributed to the writing of this book. This book also relies on my own experience, writings and research. AW

Alvarez, A. (1970). **The Savage God**. New York: Random House.

American Ass'n of Psychiatry (1987). **DSM-III-R**. New York: W.W. Norton.

Andreasen, N.C. (1984). **The Broken Brain**. New York: Harper and Row.

Battin, M.P. and Mayo, D. (Eds.) (1980). **Suicide: The Philosophical Issues**. New York: St. Martin's Press.

Berent, I. (1981). **The Algebra of Suicide**. New York: Human Sciences Press.

Bolton, I. (1983). **My Son, My Son**. Atlanta: Bolton Press.

Canada: Vital Statistics, Health Division, Statistics Canada, Ottawa.

Coleman, L. (1987). **Suicide Clusters**. Boston: Faber and Faber.

Dunne, E.J., McIntosh, J.L., & Dunne-Maxim, K. (Eds.) (1987). **Suicide and Its Aftermath**. New York: W.W. Norton.

Farberow, N.L. (Ed.) (1980). **The Many Faces of Suicide.** New York: McGraw-Hill Book Company.

Fieve, R.R. (1975). **Moodswing.** New York: Bantam Books.

Gold, M.S. (1987). **The Good News About Depression.** New York: Villard Books.

Grollman, E.A. (1988). **Suicide: Prevention, Intervention and Postvention.** Boston: Beacon Press.

Grollman, E.A. (1970). **Talking About Death.** Boston: Beacon Press.

Hendin, H. (1982). **Suicide in America.** New York: W.W. Norton.

Hewett, J.H. (1980). **After Suicide.** Philadelphia: Westminster Press.

Hinckley, J., Hinckley, J. & Sherrill, E. (1985). **Breaking Points.** Grand Rapids, MI: Chosen Books.

Klagsbrun, F. (1981). **Too Young To Die.** New York: Pocket Books.

Krementz, J. (1981). **How It Feels When A Parent Dies.** New York: Alfred A Knopf.

LeShan, E. (1976). **Learning To Say Good-bye.** New York: Avon Books.

Levin, J. & Fox J.A. (1985). **Mass Murder.** New York: Plenum Press.

Lukas, C. & Seiden, H.M. (1987). **Silent Grief.** New York: Charles Scribner's Sons.

Maris, R.W. (1981). **Pathways To Suicide.** Baltimore: Johns Hopkins University Press.

McIntosh, J.L. (1985). **Research on Suicide: A Bibliography.** Westport: Greenwood Press.

Menninger, K.A. (1938). **Man Against Himself.** New York: Harcourt, Brace & Company.

Morrison, J.R. (1981). **Your Brother's Keeper.** Chicago: Nelson-Hall.

Orbach, I. (1988). **Children Who Don't Want To Live.** San Francisco: Jossey-Bass.

Osgood, N.J. (1985). **Suicide In The Elderly.** Rockville, MD: An Aspen Publication.

Papolos, D.F. & Papolos, J. (1987). **Overcoming Depression.** New York: Harper and Row.

Pfeffer, C. (1986). **The Suicidal Child.** New York: Guilford Press.

Reiterman, T. & Jacobs, J. (1982). **Raven: The Untold Story of the Rev. Jim Jones and His People.** New York: E.P. Dutton.

Roy, A. (Ed.) (1986). **Suicide.** Baltimore: Williams & Wilkins.

Sheehan, S. (1982). **Is There No Place On Earth For Me?** Boston: Houghton Mifflin.

Shneidman, E. (1985). **Definition of Suicide.** New York: John Wiley & Sons.

Shneidman, E. (1980). **Voices of Death.** New York: Harper & Row.

Stengel, E. (1958). **Attempted Suicide.** Westport: Greenwood Press.

Torrey, E.F. (1983). **Surviving Schizophrenia.** New York: Harper & Row.

United States National Center for Health Statistics, Vital Statistics Mortality Branch.

Wender, P.H. & Klein, D.F. (1981). **Mind, Mood and Medicine.** New York: New American Library.

Wekstein, L. (1979). **Handbook of Suicidology.** New York: Brunner/Mazel.

Winokur, G. (1981). **Depression: The Facts.** New York: Oxford University Press.

Winokur, G. & Clayton, P. (1986). **The Medical Basis of Psychiatry.** Philadelphia: W.B. Saunders.

WROBLESKI'S PUBLICATIONS

Wrobleski, A. "The Suicide Survivors Grief Group." **Omega: Journal of Death and Dying,** Vol. 15(2), 1984-85.

Chigier, E. (Ed.) **Grief and Bereavement in Contemporary Society,** London: Freund Publishing. Wrobleski, A., McIntosh, J. "Problems of Suicide Survivors: An Exploratory Investigation."

Wrobleski, A., McIntosh, J., "Problems of Suicide Survivors: A Survey Report." **Israel Journal of Psychiatry,** Fall, Tel Aviv, Israel, 1987.

Corr, C., Pacholski, R. (Eds.) 1987, **Death: Completion and Discovery,** Ass'n Death Education & Counseling, Lakewood, OH. Wrobleski, A. McIntosh, J. "Responses of Suicide Survivors."

Wrobleski, A. "Mutual Help Groups for Those Bereaved by Suicide." **Bereavement Care,** V 15(2), London, England, 1987.

Dunne, E., McIntosh, J., Dunne-Maxim, K. (Eds.) 1987, **Suicide and Its Aftermath,** W.W. Norton & Co., New York. Appel, Y., & Wrobleski, A. "Self-Help & Support Groups."

McIntosh, J., & Wrobleski A., "Grief Reactions Among Suicide Survivors: a Comparison," **Death Studies,** Jan. 1988.

Summary and Research on Alleged Imitation of Suicide by Teenagers

David Phillips, Ph.D.

The belief that suicide is highly imitative arose with studies done by David Phillips, Ph.D., of the Sociology Department of the University of California at San Diego. His studies purported that additional suicides followed various events such as front page news of suicide, and even after a fictional representation of suicide on a soap opera. His methodology has been challenged, however. He did other studies with the same results; he found extra suicides after publicity or stories about suicide. Phillips began reporting his work in 1973.

Center for Disease Control (CDC)

In a paper presented at the American Association of Suicidology in Atlanta on May 27, 1987, Patrick O'Carroll, M.D., of CDC said "Problems we have run into in trying to investigate and find out about the phenomenon of suicide clusters is...there is no standard definition of cluster...in fact, the only clusters we are aware of at CDC are those that happen to be identified by the media...There is no formal surveillance system in effect in the United States that I am aware of that identifies suicide clusters at this time...

"Finally," he concluded "suicide is rare...the ones that I am aware of...involve clusters of two or three individuals. And it is difficult to draw very powerful conclusions from an examination of two or three individuals who committed suicide and comparing them to two or three other individuals who did not."

David Shaffer, M.D. and Marilyn Gould, Ph.D.

In September, 1986, the **New England Journal of Medicine** published Shaffer and Gould's study claiming that as a result of the airing of three television programs about teenage suicide there were eighty extra imitative suicides. This study received immense publicity, and exploded on the nation. The conclusion was that suicide should not be depicted nor even spoken about to teenagers. (**New England Journal of Medicine**, 9/11/86).

Replication Attempts

Exactly a year later in the same journal, David Phillips, Ph.D, reported he had tried and failed to replicate the Shaffer-Gould study. "Using their methods, we studied teenage suicides in California and Pennsylvania before and after the television broadcast of the same three films...there was no evidence of an increase in teenage suicides after the films were shown...We conclude that it is premature to be concerned about possibly fatal effects of fictional televised films about suicide." (**New England Journal of Medicine**, 9/24/87).

Gould and Shaffer tried and failed to replicate their own results, and stated "The impact of the television broadcasts of fictional stories featuring suicidal behavior appears less widespread than we had originally proposed" (**Suicide and Life-Threatening Behavior**, Vol. 18(1), Spring, 1988).

Alan L. Berman, Ph.D., reported "In contrast to Gould and Shaffer's study, and in support of Phillip's replication, the present study found no support for the hypothesis that suicidal behavior by fictional television characters leads to an increase in suicides by youthful viewers" (**American Journal of Psychiatry**, 145:8, August 1988).

Ronald Kessler, Ph.D., et al, studied not only the 1973-1979 period of previous research (of Shaffer and Gould), but also 1980 - 1984. They report, "The authors found no significant association between newscasts and subsequent teenage suicides over the 1973-1984. Although teenage suicides increased after newscasts in 1973-1980, the authors identify reasons why this increase is not consistent with an imitative effect of television. Furthermore, during 1981-1984 teenage suicides decreased after newscasts about suicide." (**American Journal of Psychiatry,** 145:11, November, 1988).

Other resources by Adina Wrobleski

Booklets:

Suicide: Questions and Answers 3rd Ed. 1989
Suicide: The Danger Signs, 2nd Ed. 1986
Suicide: Your Child Has Died 3rd Ed. 1987

Tape Cassettes of Speeches:

Suicide: We Are All Victims
Suicide: A Teenage Tragedy

Newsletter:

AFTERWORDS: A Letter About Suicide and Suicide Grief.

Quantity prices available
For ordering information write or call:

Adina Wrobleski
AFTERWORDS
5124 Grove Street
Minneapolis, MN 55436
(612) 929-6448

INDEX